Do the Planet

by Claire Daniel
illustrations by Fian Arroyo

Harcourt Brace & Company

Orlando Atlanta Austin Boston San Francisco Chicago Dallas New York Toronto London

A spacecraft landed in back of Dave's house. The hatch came open, and a space crab ran out.

"Come, Dave," the space crab said. The space crab grasped Dave's hand, and Dave went in the spacecraft.

Dave came face-to-face with Grand Crab. Grand Crab said, "Don't be afraid. I am glad you are here."

Then the spacecraft blasted away with a flash!

Grand Crab said, "Look at the mess people make! Look at the trash in the lake! Look at the cans, glass, and paper people waste! Trash and waste make me sad. They make me mad!! Help me save your planet!"

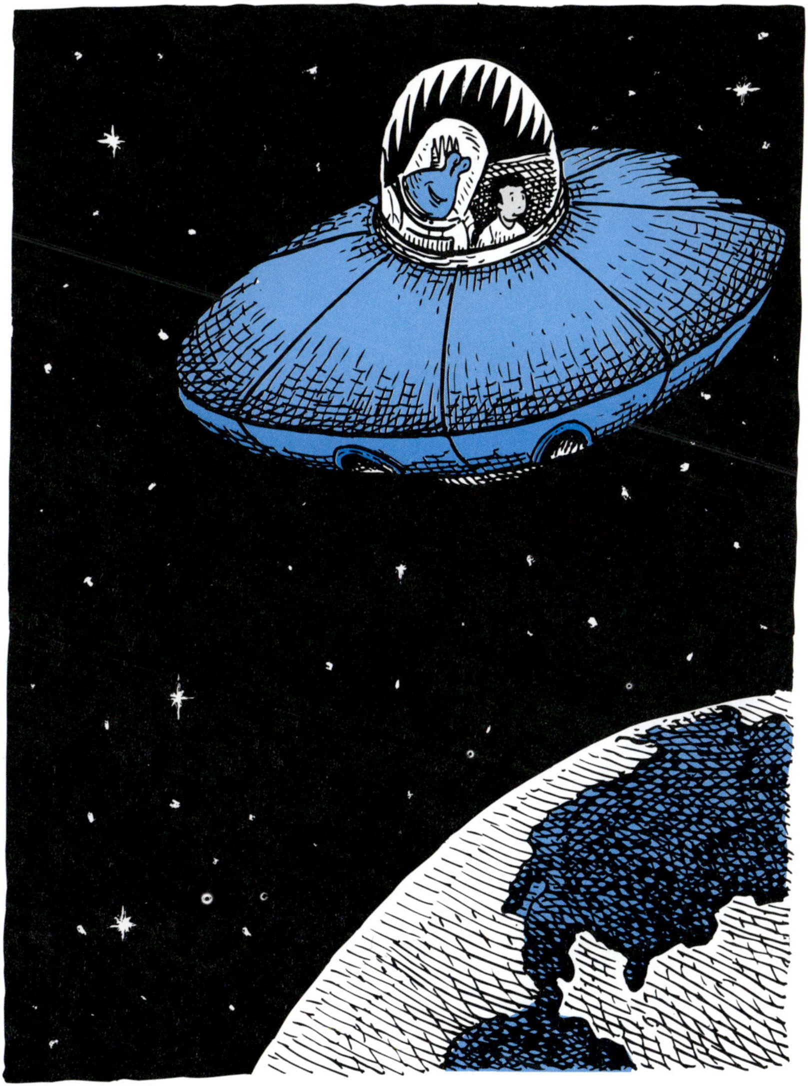

Dave made a face. "I am just a boy. How can I save the planet?"

"What will happen if you stand back and wait? Dave, don't wait until it's too late. My planet did, and now my crabs stay in space. We don't have a place to live," stated Grand Crab.

"It's not too late for YOUR planet, Dave."

9

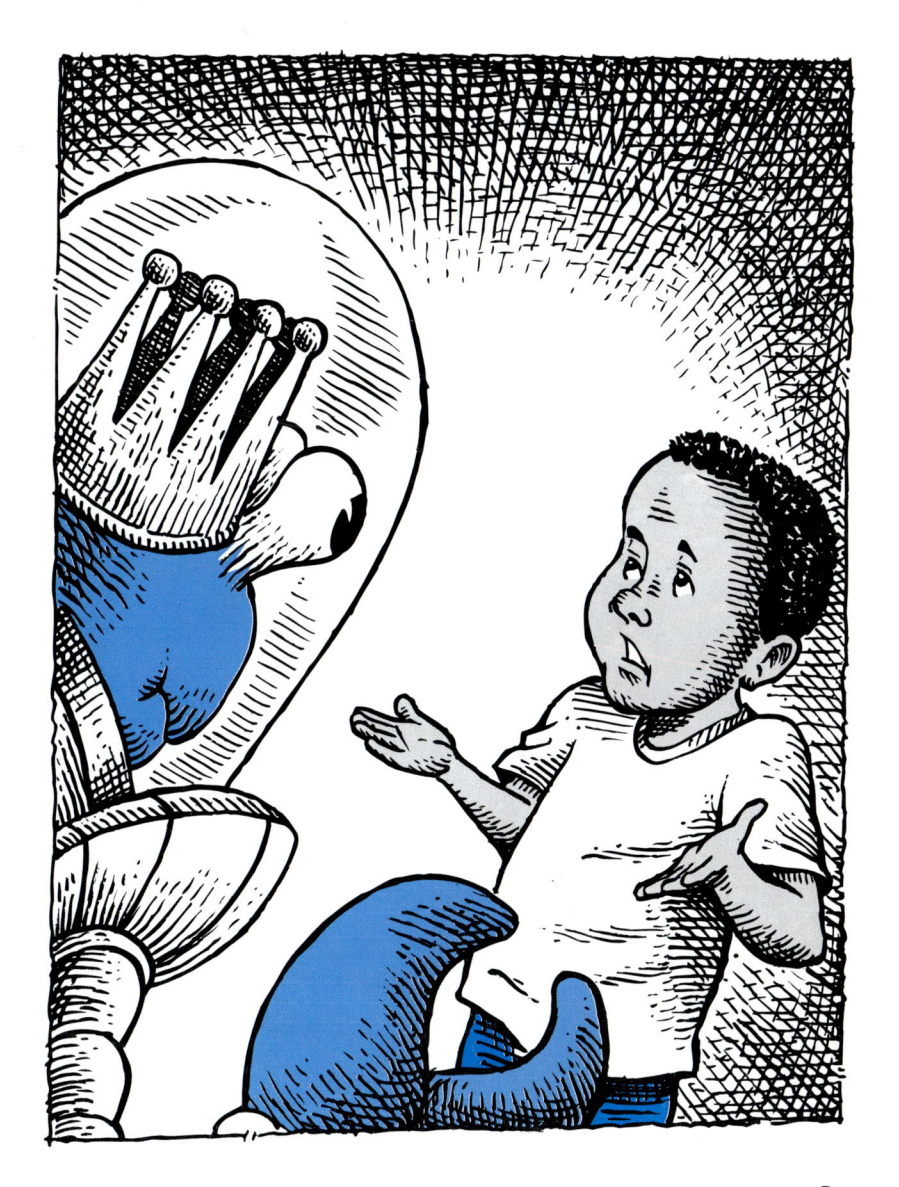

"But wait! What can I do? Wait! Wait!" wailed Dave.

"People can change, Dave!" Grand Crab said as his spacecraft faded away.

"Wake up, Dave," Dad said.

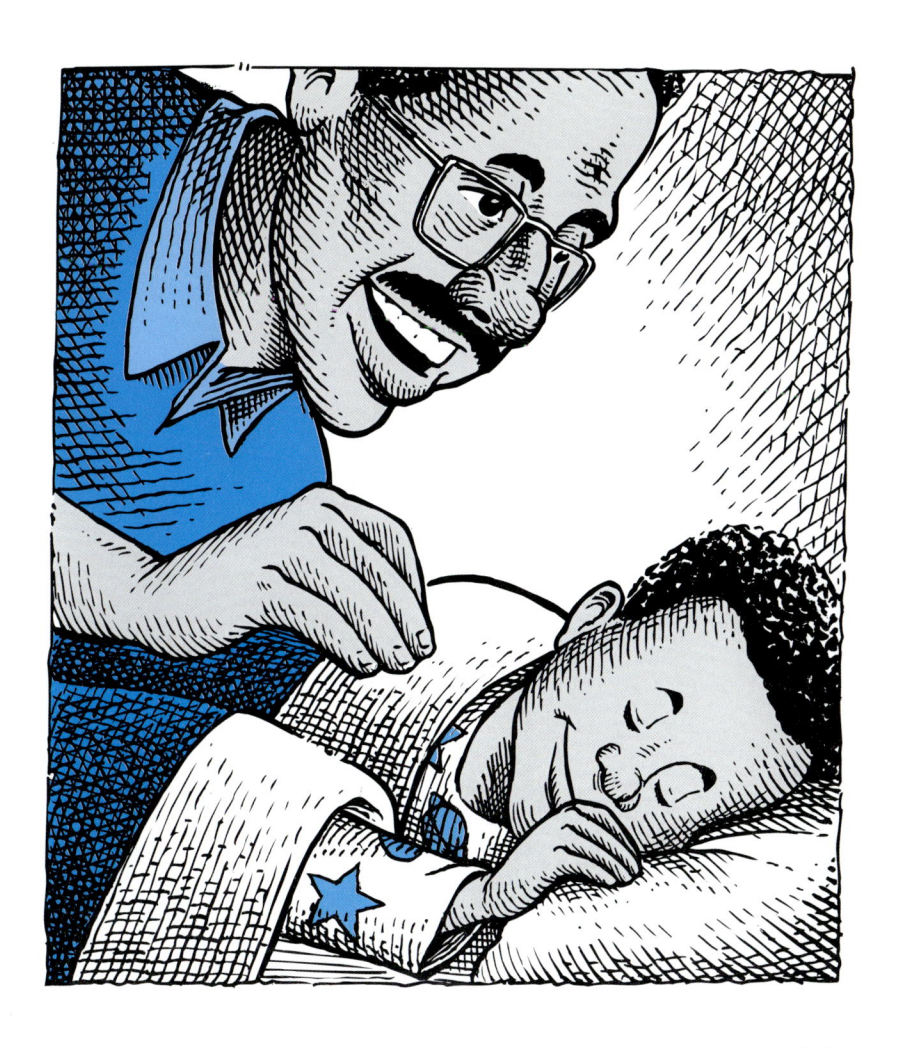

"Dad! Dad!" said Dave.
"We must save our planet!
Can you help?"

Dave and his dad made lots of changes. They asked people to change. Dave's pals helped, too.

Dave's dad talked to his class at the school where he worked. Dave's mom saved paper.

Dave's classmates saved cans and glass. Lots of people came and took away the trash at the lake. They planted grass. The place looked beautiful!

"It will stay this way!" said Dave.

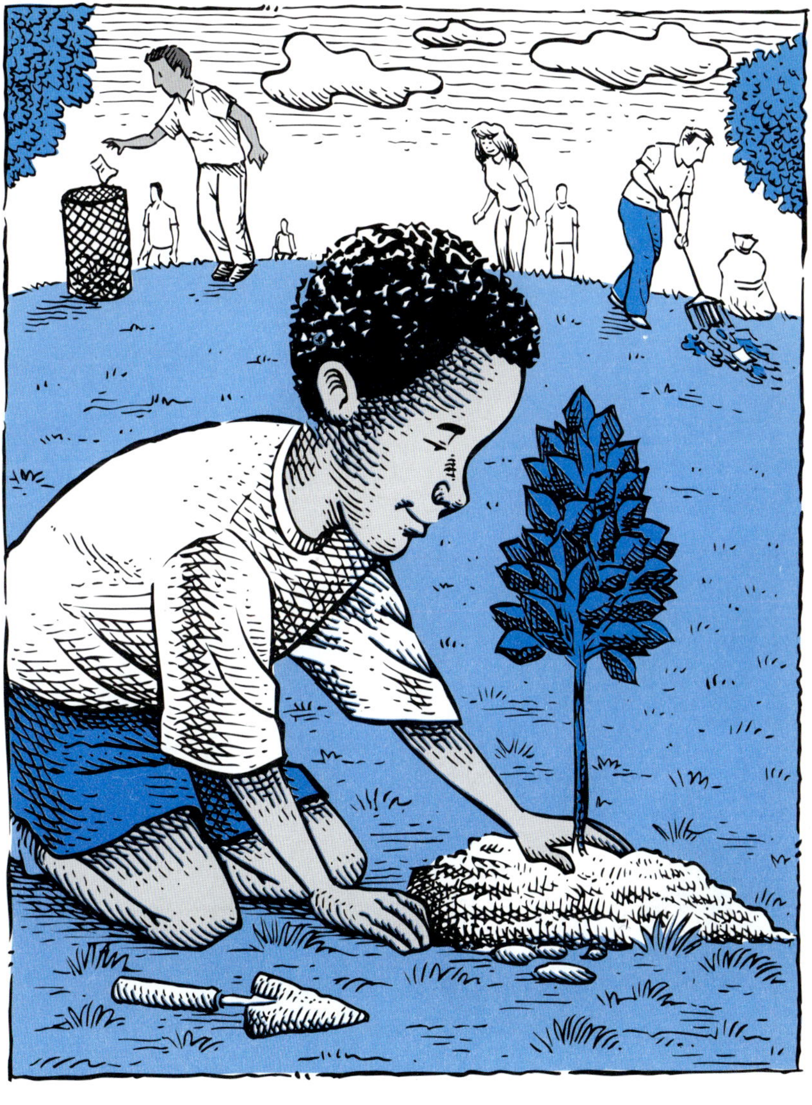

Dave was glad. And Grand Crab would be, too.